My affinity for pr[...]
as a young boy [...]
My mom had se[...]
cookers and often used th[...]
to prepare many of her m[...]
watch the ritual and volu[...]
official taster of her mout[...]
practically everyday.

From this passion, I've in[...]
600,000 cooks to similar [...]
with modern pressure co[...]
electronic brains.

Almost an entire generati[...]
pleasure of pressure cook[...]
speed of the pressure coo[...]
replaces the pressure cool[...]

Thanks to safe modern pr[...]
vengeance and with the n[...]
easier or safer. These pre[...]
many new models offer u[...]

Until now there hasn't be[...]
pressure settings. My boc[...]
childhood favorites with t[...]
more than try a few of th[...]

My goal is to pass along t[...]
pressure cooking can be. [...]
easy recipes are unsurpas[...]

Bob Warden

This book is dedicated to my mother

Avonelle Warden
1912 - 1984
who taught me to love to cook

And, To Pam Falk
who inspires me to keep on cooking

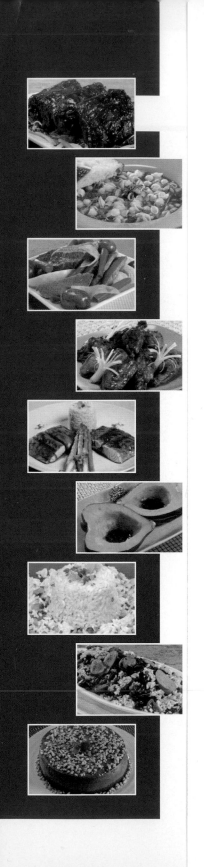

The Essentials of Pressure Cooking

How pressure cookers work

Why does a pressure cooker cook up to three times faster than an open steamer or ordinary pot? It's very simple. Steam transfers heat to food faster than water and steam, under pressure transfers it's heat even faster than that. Set most pressure cookers to high and save up to 2/3 cooking time. Most pressure cookers have either low (7-1/2 lbs/sq") or high (15 lbs/sq") settings but many modern pressure cookers have up to four settings, typically 20, 40, 60 and 80 kilopascals. The abbreviation for kilopascals is either kps or kPa. High pressure is translated to a 80 kps setting and low pressure converts to either 20 or 40 kps. Please know that all times and settings are approximate. The size of the food pieces and the altitude above sea level in which you cook will alter the speed. Low pressure settings are useful for quickly prepared food such as vegetables and fish. See the cooking time charts in this book for recommended pressure settings and cooking times. Current electric pressure cookers will set the pressure and time with the push of a button and give you the option of delaying food preparation time. The cooker will start when you ask, cook to your specifications, turn itself off when finished and keep your meal warm until you're ready to eat. How much easier could it be?

What foods cook best in a pressure cooker

Almost any food can be cooked (steamed under pressure) in a pressure cooker though it's particularly advantageous to cook beans, tougher cuts of meat, soups, stews, chilies and risottos because of the flavor infusion and the fraction of the time to cook compared to other methods. Cooking under pressure breaks down tough connective tissues of meat and makes even the toughest, inexpensive cut of meat tender and delicious. When meats are browned first in the cooker, extra layers of flavor are added from the Maillard and caramelizing processes. When vegetables, herbs and spices are added they become infused with even more flavor in a way not possible in conventional cooking. Cooking under pressure is also more healthful, similar to steaming. Flavor and water soluble nutrients aren't boiled away. Fresh corn on the cob can be steamed in just three minutes (on the trivet or steamer basket) and never touch the water. I've not found a cooking method where steamed carrots retain more of their flavor.

How to adapt conventional recipes for a pressure cooker

Almost any recipe that requires long and slow cooking, or braising can be adapted for the pressure cooker by dividing by three. Braising shows off the most significant difference because there's no loss of moisture resulting in a thinner but more flavorful sauce. You may thicken the sauce with a roux (flour and water) or slurry of cornstarch and water right in the pressure cooker at the same time as the meat cools.

Safety

Be sure and read the manufacturer's directions before using your pressure cooker. Follow the recommendations for cleaning and maintenance. Modern pressure cookers are made to high safety standards but you're responsible for operating, cleaning and maintaining your cooker properly. With proper use and care, modern pressure cookers offer the best possible protection and should last many years.

Bob's Ten Favorite Pressure Cooker Recipes

My Mom's Pot Roast

My Mom made this pot roast at least once a week for dinner, which is eaten at noon on the farm. Growing up on a farm we ate three big meals a day, breakfast at six after our morning chores, dinner and then supper whenever our evening chores were done. Two additional cold lunches were served mid-morning and mid-afternoon in the field. We call pot roast comfort food now but back then we needed every fork-tender, succulent piece just to maintain our energy.

Serves: 6

My Mom's Pot Roast

4 pounds beef chuck roast (add ten minutes cooking time for frozen)

4 cloves garlic peeled and cut length-wise into thin pointy slices

6 tablespoons oil

pepper to taste

1 cup onions, chopped

1/2 cup celery, chopped

1/2 cup carrots, chopped

1/2 cup leeks, sliced thin

1 cup dry red wine (use a good quality wine)

2-1/2 cups beef bouillon

1 sprig rosemary

2 bay leaves

3 medium carrots, cut into two inch chunks

1 pound medium thin-skinned potatoes, cut into large chunks

3 large sweet onions, cut into large chunks

2 tablespoons all purpose flour

2 tablespoons sweet butter, mashed into flour at room temperature

With a pairing knife make incisions into the roast a bit deeper than the length of your garlic slices, about 3/4 of an inch. Push the garlic slices into the incisions so that the meat seals around the garlic. Be careful to distribute the garlic evenly around the whole surface of the roast. Season the outside with salt and pepper. Set cooker to brown and heat the oil until very hot. With the lid off sear the meat on all sides, until very brown and almost crusty. This browning step will provide over 300 new flavors and aromas through the Mailard process and mouth watering caramelization of the sugars in the meat.

Remove the roast and place in a dish deep enough to capture the juices that run while it rests. Add onions, celery, carrots and leeks. Sauté long enough to brown the carrots and leeks, about 4-5 minutes. We're adding even more flavor now. Next, deglaze with the red wine and reduce for 2 minutes, scraping the bottom of the cooker to release all the browned flavors.

Add the beef stock, bay leaves and rosemary. Return the roast to the cooker, lock the lid in place and set the cooker to high, 80kps for 60 minutes. Let the pressure drop naturally, about ten minutes. Remove the lid and this roast should be ready to melt in your mouth. If it's not quite done enough return it to the cooker and pressure cook for another 10 minutes on high. Use fast-release and remove the lid. Add the carrots, potatoes and onions. Replace the lid, lock in place and set cooker on high for five minutes. Reduce pressure with quick-release.

Remove the roast and place with the vegetables on a serving platter. To thicken the gravy (with lid off) set the cooker to brown and add the sweet butter and flour mixture. Bring to a simmer, stirring constantly until gravy reaches your desired consistency. Pour gravy into gravy boat or pour it directly over your roast and vegetables and serve. Yummy!!

Bob's "Best of the Best" Short Ribs

100 MINUTES
80 KPS **HIGH**

I spent about two years testing every braised short rib recipe I could find from celebrity chefs to Joy of Cooking. The secrets I discovered in every one of these recipes can be applied to every pressure cooker or oven-braised meat dish. Always brown the meat until crisp and then set aside and brown the aromatic mirpoix vegetables thoroughly. This essential browning of the meat then the carrots, leeks onions, shallots, and celery adds hundreds of flavors to the final dish. The only exception is to never brown garlic because it turns bitter. A quick light sweating is all that's needed.

To create even more flavors deglaze now with alcohol. My favorite is a full-bodied red wine for most dishes. Many flavors created by the browning process are alcohol and not water-soluble. Adding wine, rum brandy, beer and other flavors allow us to capture these molecules for a taste that would otherwise be lost. I've found that pressure cooked-braised meats come out far tastier and more moist that even 5-7 hour oven braises. You'll love this recipe served on risotto.

Serves: 6

Bob's "Best of the Best" Short Ribs

12 - 4 inch bone-in beef short ribs
    uniform in size

2 cups white flour

Salt and pepper to taste

1 whole onion, chopped

2 cups leeks, sliced 1/4 inch thick

Two large carrots, thinly sliced

1 stalk celery, sliced 1/4 inch thick

2 cloves garlic, thinly sliced

1 cup good quality red wine
    I like Cabernet or Merlot

6 cups veal stock (chicken or beef
    can be substituted in a pinch

2 sprigs fresh rosemary
    (1 tbs of dry can be substituted)

The zest of one whole lemon

A fine grater works perfect

Season the ribs with salt and pepper and drench them in the flour. Shake off the excess flour so that a fine powder remains. This flour will help in the browning process and will later provide some thickening to the sauce as it reduces. Set the cooker to brown and add the oil. When the oil is just smoking hot add the ribs in batches, turning until they're brown on each side. I often use another fry pan on my stovetop to speed up the process of browning the meat and vegetables.

Set the ribs aside and add the onion, leeks, carrots and celery. Let them sauté until golden brown. Deglaze the pan or pans with the red wine, scraping the bottom to get all the browned bits dissolved in the wine. Reduce the wine to half.

Return the ribs and all the remaining ingredients to the cooker. You'll need to stack the ribs in two layers and have them just about covered with stock. Lock the lid in place and set on high, 80kps for 100 minutes.

Normally in an oven-braise I'd cook these tough old ribs at 250 degrees F for 5 hours, or 300 minutes. With the pressure cooker the ribs are done in 1/3 the time. Remember we want to break down that tough connective tissue holding the meat to the bone until it turns into a stock flavored gelatin that melts in our mouth.

Carefully remove the ribs and place on a platter and cover with foil. Hold them warm in an oven at 200 degrees F. With a fine colander strain the vegetables from the sauce and discard. They've given up all their flavor to the sauce and you should have about 6 or 7 cups of liquid. Reserve one cup for pouring over the ribs. Use the remaining stock to make risotto.

Place one cup of cooked risotto on each plate. Place two to three ribs per person on the risotto, pour over the reserved stock and serve. You'll get rave reviews.

Perfect Beef Stew in 20 Minutes

I love mouth-watering beef stew, especially when it's super tender. The pressure cooker is the fastest and surest way to achieve the most succulent beef. I never buy stew meat that is already cut and packaged because I find that it's often a mixture of trimmings of several different cuts of beef and it's seldom cut uniformly. Buy chuck or round roast at a reasonable price and cut the meat yourself into uniform cubes that will cook evenly.

Serves: 6

20 MINUTES
80 KPS **HIGH**

2 pounds chuck or round roast
   cut into 1-1/2 in cubes

2 pounds (about 16) medium new red
   or white potatoes coarsely chopped
   (bite size)

3 large carrots
   peeled and cut into bite size chunks

2 large garlic cloves, minced

1/2 pound white mushrooms
   cut into about four pieces each

1 14-ounce can chopped tomatoes

1/2 cup beef bouillon

1/2 cup red wine

1 tablespoon Worcestershire sauce

2 bay leaves

1 sprig fresh thyme, or 1/2 tsp of dry

1 teaspoon dry mustard

1/8 teaspoon ground allspice

1 package frozen and defrosted petite peas
   and pearl onions

1/2 package frozen French-style
   green beans

1/4 cup parsley, finely chopped

salt and pepper to taste

Place all the ingredients except the peas, onions, green beans, parsley and salt and pepper in the cooker and stir together. Lock the lid in place and set to high, 80 kps for 20 minutes. Let the pressure drop naturally, about 10 to 12 minutes.

The beef should now be fork-tender. If it's not, don't be afraid to cook it for an additional five minutes, again letting the pressure drop naturally. Stir in the remaining ingredients and simmer with the lid off for about 5 minutes. Season with salt and pepper to taste. You can make this recipe in advance because it tastes even better after the flavors meld overnight!

Barbecue Ribs

We make these ribs every time we show a pressure cooker during our TV shows.
It's simple because all we do is throw in the ribs, add in a prepared barbecue sauce and season to taste.
Finger-Licken good!

Serves: 6

4 pounds pork baby back ribs
 or country style ribs
1 16-ounce bottle barbecue sauce,
 your favorite
1/4 cup water, to thin the
 barbecue sauce a bit

20 MINUTES
80 KPS **HIGH**

Cut the ribs in sections to fit the cooker and position to standing on their edge. Add he barbecue sauce and 1/4 cup of water. Lock the lid in place and set the cooker on igh, 80kps for 20 minutes. Let the pressure release naturally then open the cooker nd check for tenderness.

like my barbecue ribs tender but everyone has their own preference of how well lone they like them cooked. You may want to pressure cook your ribs up to 15 minutes more if you like them to fall off the bone like I do. Experiment to taste and ook them for that time in the future.

Chicken Cacciatore (Hunter Style)

Generally cacciatore recipes call for cut-up chicken but this whole chicken cacciatore recipe is the one we like to demonstrate in the pressure cooker on our TV shows.

Serves: 6

20 MINUTES
80 KPS **HIGH**

2 each 3 to 5 pound chickens (you can cut them up if you wish, but they will easily pull apart when done)

2 tablespoons olive oil

1 cup onions, chopped

2 cloves garlic, thinly sliced

8 small white mushrooms, thinly sliced

1/3 cup dry white wine

1 28-ounce can crushed tomatoes

1 teaspoon salt

1/4 teaspoon black pepper

1 tablespoon minced parsley

2 cups cooked white rice (See basic white rice recipe)

Set the cooker to brown and heat the olive oil to almost smoking. Add the chickens in one at a time, or a few pieces at a time and turn until golden brown. Set aside on a large plate that collects the juice. Now add the onion, garlic, and mushrooms and cook for 2 minutes to a browned chicken, including the juice. Set the cooker on high, 80 kps for 20 minutes. Let the pressure release naturally about 10 minutes. Unlock and remove the cover. Transfer to a serving platter, garnish with parsley and serve with the rice.

Fifteen Minute Turkey Chili

Of course the pressure cooker is great for cooking dried beans fast, but when you want to have a meal on the table quickly, canned beans and prepared sausage is one of my standby tricks of the trade.

Serves: 6

tablespoon olive oil

pounds ground turkey

pound smoked turkey sausage cut into 1/2 inch rounds and further cut into four pieces

cups onions coarsely chopped

tablespoon whole cumin seeds

3 cup white wine

14 1/2-ounce can chicken broth

14-ounce can red kidney beans

14-ounce can white navy beans or cannellini beans

1 10-ounce can green enchilada sauce

1/2 teaspoon mild chili powder to taste

1/4 teaspoon ground cinnamon to taste

2 large red bell peppers seeded and coarsely chopped

1 15-ounce can diced tomatoes

2 cloves garlic, finely minced

2 tablespoons quick cooking polenta or cornmeal to thicken the chili

sour cream, for garnish

fresh cilantro, finely minced for garnish

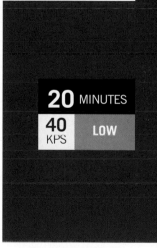

20 MINUTES

40 KPS · LOW

et the cooker to brown, add oil and sausage. Brown the sausage well on all sides and set aside. dd the ground turkey and stir a few minutes to break up clumps, until it's no longer pink. Add he onions and cumin and stir until well blended. Add the white wine and broth and deglaze the ottom of the pan with a wooden spoon to include the delicious browned bits of meat from the ottom of the pan. Stir in the browned sausage, beans, enchilada sauce, chili powder, cinnamon, nd bell peppers. Pour the chopped tomatoes and garlic on top and do not stir.

ock the lid in place, set the cooker on low, 40 kps for 15 minutes. Quick-release the pressure, set he cooker to brown and stir in the polenta, tomatoes and garlic. Cook until the mixture thickens r a couple of minutes and season to taste. Garnish with sour cream and cilantro.

Pulled Pork

90 MINUTES
80 KPS **HIGH**

1 4 to 5 pound pork shoulder or butt

1 14 1/2-ounce can chicken broth

For the barbecue, if desired select your favorite prepared or home made barbecue sauce

Someone told me that this is becoming the most popular sandwich in America after the hamburger and grilled cheese. To get a tough pork shoulder or butt tender enough to pull, you would have to cook this by another conventional method, about 8 to 9 hours, 540 minutes. To achieve the same result in your pressure cooker, divide 540 by 3 and you get 180 minutes, 3 hours. To cut that time in half, cut the shoulder or butt in half and arrange it side by side with a spacer in between. A large carrot works fine. The pork will cook more than twice as fast if half as thick. According to my food science textbook, every inch of thickness can double the cooking time. Keep your pieces no more than two inches thick and you will be pulling pork in 90 minutes every time. Because I like to emphasize the flavor of the pork when not making a sauce, this recipe calls for only chicken stock for cooking. If you like a less neutral tasting pulled pork, add onions, garlic and your favorite spices to the chicken stock, or adapt your favorite slow cooking recipe by cutting the cooking time to one-third.

Serves: 12

Cut the pork into pieces no more than 2 inches thick. Put the pork and chicken broth in the cooker, separating the pieces with a spacer such as a carrot. Lock the lid in place and set the cooker on high, 80 kps for 90 minutes. Let the pressure release naturally, open the lid and check to see if the pork will shred easily with a fork. If not, lock the lid in place an cook on high pressure for an additional 20 minutes. You can quick-release the pressure.

Remove the pork to a large cutting board and shred with a fork or pull apart with tongs. Return the pulled pork to the cooker and set it to warm with lid on until ready to serve.

Quick Rice Pudding with Sun-Dr[ied]

This is a great holiday dessert. On our Iowa farm we often ate rice pudding for breakfast. It's a great high energy pick-me-up. We'd add our favorite dried and fresh fruits to the hot rice. We dried almost every fruit from our orchard but the store bought dried cranberries Mom got were my favorite. You can also make this recipe in advance, store covered in the refrigerator and serve at the last minute.

Serves: 6

cup rice, short grain

tablespoons sweet butter

cups water

14oz can 2 percent
    evaporated milk

2 teaspoon ground cinnamon

4 teaspoon nutmeg
    freshly grated is best

1/2 cup dried cranberrie[s]
    or raisins, cherries,
    chopped apricots, e[tc.]

1/2 cup sweetened
    condensed milk

1 tsp vanilla extract
    or pulp from one vani[lla]

Emergency Chicken or Pork Dinner with Sauce

One of the great things about a pressure cooker is that you can cook food directly from the freezer without thawing it first. I keep frozen chicken breasts, pork chops, whole chickens and chuck roasts on-hand for quick, emergency meals.

For this particular recipe you can use frozen chicken breasts or frozen pork chops. My rule of thumb is if it's frozen, add ten minutes for every inch of thickness. For 1/2 inch frozen chicken breasts or pork chops your meal is ready in 15 minutes. If they're fresh, cook them for only 10 minutes. You can use your favorite canned sauce or gravy with this recipe.

Serves: 6

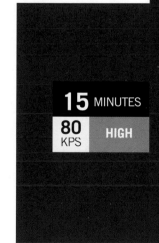

15 MINUTES

80 KPS HIGH

4 to 6 1/2 inch frozen or
    fresh chicken breasts
    or pork chops

1 15-ounce can
    tomato sauce or
    your favorite gravy

salt and pepper to taste

[S]et cooker to brown and melt butter. Stir in rice and [a]dd water, evaporated milk, cinnamon and nutmeg. [_] minutes, lock cover into place making sure the relea[se_] [W]hen done, quick-release pressure, remove lid and st[ir in] [m]ilk and vanilla. Let stand for 5 minutes with cover [_] [ab]sorbed and serve in either ramekins or bowls. Gar[nish]

[A]dd the meat and the tomato sauce or gravy and set the cooker to high, 80kps for 15 minutes. Cover and press start. Let the pressure release naturally, about 5 minutes and place breasts or chops on a plate and cover with sauce or gravy. Season to taste, garnish with scallion flowers and serve.

Glazed Carr...

6 large carrots, peeled
1 can chicken broth
1 teaspoon Italian seasoning

5 MINUTES
40 KPS **MEDIUM**

Slice the carrots into 1/2 in
chicken broth and Italian s
place in the cooker. Lock t
medium, 40 kps for 5 minu

Remove the basket of carrots and save the broth
recipes. Set the cooker to brown and return the
brown sugar and butter. Stir the mixture togeth
with butter and the sugar has dissolved. Sauté f
start to turn a golden brown.

Serve the carrots piping hot as a side dish to you
undoubtedly be the best carrots you've had in y

SOUPS & STOCKS

Pasta Fazool

They say there is no Fazool like and old Italian Fazool or, Fagioli. It's an old classic dish of pasta and beans with good Italian flavorings. Don't forget to drizzle with extra virgin olive oil. Always buy good olive oil!

Serves: 6

1-1/2 cups dried white cannellini beans or white navy beans

3 tablespoons
  extra virgin olive oil

4 ounces pancetta,
  or proscuitto, chopped

1 large onion, chopped

1 large carrot, chopped

2 stalks celery, chopped

1 clove garlic, minced

1 sprig rosemary, minced

1 pinch red pepper flakes

1/4 cup fresh basil, chopped,
  or, 1 tsp dried basil

1 28 ounce can
  Italian plum tomatoes, chopped

3 cups chicken broth

1-1/2 cups small shell pasta,
  or small rotini or orecchiette

salt and pepper to taste

Parmesan cheese or Asiago,
grated for garnish

extra virgin olive oil,
drizzled for traditional flavor

20 MINUTES

80 KPS   HIGH

oak beans overnight, or use the quick soak method. Set cooker to brown and heat il. Add onion, carrots and pancetta or prosciutto. Sauté for two minutes. Add arlic, beans, 1/2 of rosemary, basil, red pepper flakes, tomatoes and broth. Lock lid place. Set cooker to high, 80 kps for 15 minutes. Let pressure drop naturally.

pen lid and stir in pasta. Set cooker to brown and cook for 7 minutes, or until asta is tender. Salt and pepper to taste. Serve in deep soup bowls. Garnish with rizzle of olive oil, rosemary and grated cheese.

TENDER
& DELICIOUS

Corned Beef and Cabbage

A delicious dish that usually takes hours to tenderize. Now you can do it in under an hour.

Serves: 8

2 pounds corned beef, trimmed of fat

3 cups chicken broth

3 cups water

4 bay leaves

8 peppercorns

1/4 cup apple cider vinegar

8 medium new red or white potatoes left whole

8 cups coarsely sliced cabbage

40 MINUTES

80 KPS **HIGH**

Place beef in pressure cooker. Add stock, water, bay leaves, peppercorns, and vinegar. Lock lid in place, set to high pressure, 80 kps for 40 minutes. Let pressure drop naturally for 10 minutes and quick-release any remaining pressure.

Add potatoes. Lock lid in place, set cooker to high for 8 minutes. Quick-release pressure. Add cabbage. Cook loosely covered (don't lock lid) until cabbage is crisp-tender, 5 to 6 minutes. Transfer beef, potatoes, and cabbage to a serving platter and garnish with parsley if you like.

Sweet-n-Sour Chicken

In just a few minutes dinner can be on the table with this quick and easy recipe.

Coat chicken thighs in flour. Set cooker to brown, add oil and heat until almost smoking. Add chicken and brown evenly on all sides. Combine pineapple juice and remaining ingredients, with the exception of the pineapple chunks, cornstarch, and water. Pour over chicken. Lock lid and set cooker to high, 80 kps for 10 minutes.

Quick-release pressure. Remove chicken and vegetables. Mix cornstarch into the cold water until smooth slurry is formed. Whisk into hot liquid in cooker. Set cooker to brown and cook, stirring until mixture boils and thickens. Salt and pepper to taste.

Add pineapple chunks and pour over chicken. Serve over hot cooked rice.

3 pounds chicken thighs

1/2 cup flour

1 tablespoon vegetable oil

1 20-ounce can pineapple chunks, drained, reserve liquid

1-1/2 cups reserved pineapple juice, add water if necessary

1/2 stalk celery, sliced 1/4 inch thick

1 red or green bell pepper, seeded and cut into 3/4 inch chunks

1/4 cup brown sugar

1/2 cup cider vinegar

2 tablespoons soy sauce

1 tablespoon ketchup

1/2 teaspoon Worcestershire sauce

1/4 teaspoon ground ginger

2 tablespoons cornstarch

2 tablespoons cold water

salt and pepper to taste

Serves 6

PARTY TIME FAVORITES

M
p

In
in
ha
1-
u
sa
p
m

R
d
b
in

Hummus

Hummus made from freshly cooked chickpeas is delicious and easy. It's made perfect every time with the pressure cooker and is a great party food or appetizer. Serve with warm pita bread.

Combine the chickpeas, water, oil and salt in the cooker. Lock lid and set to high, 80 kps for 35 minutes. Let the pressure drop naturally, about 15 minutes. Remove the lid and drain the chickpeas into a colander, over a bowl to reserve the cooking liquid. Cool the chickpeas to room temperature. You can run cold water over them if you're in a hurry.

For the Hummus:

Add chickpeas to a food processor, tahini paste, 1/2 the lemon juice and lightly salt. With the motor running on low, slowly add some of the reserved cooking liquid until you have a smooth thick consistency. Taste and blend in more lemon and salt and pepper to taste.

Serve immediately or keep covered in the refrigerator for up to one week. Serve with warm pita bread.

3 cups dried chickpeas

2 quarts water, or enough to cover chickpeas by two inches

2 tablespoons vegetable oil to control foaming

1/2 teaspoon salt

For the hummus:

2 cloves garlic, minced

6 tablespoons sesame tahini

1/2 cup lemon juice, added to taste

salt and pepper to taste

1/2 cup chickpea cooking liquid

Serves 10

SEAFOOD

My Favorite Steamed Salmon

Steamed salmon is the purest way to show off the natural taste of salmon. In this recipe we're adding a tangy red wine glaze to delight the palate.

Serves: 4

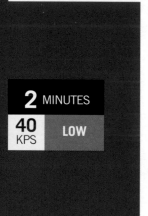

2 MINUTES

40 KPS LOW

4 salmon filets, one inch thick
1/2 cup onions,
    sliced into 1/4 inch slices
1/2 cup dry white wine
1/2 cup vegetable broth
2 sprigs thyme
2 sprigs parsley
salt and pepper to taste

For the glaze:
1 tablespoon brown sugar
1/2 cup grapefruit juice
1/2 cup dry red wine
1 tablespoon tomato paste
1 tablespoon sweet butter
1 grapefruit, peeled sectioned and
    skin removed for garnish

Add onion, wine, stock, thyme and parsley to the cooker. Place the salmon in a steamer rack and put the steamer in the cooker. Lock th lid in place, set the cooker to low, 40 kps and set timer for 2 minutes. Release the pressure naturally. The salmon should be just medium, 150 F if checked with a thermometer.

While the salmon is cooking prepare the glaze. Combine the sugar, grapefruit juice, red wine and tomato paste. Bring to a simmer over high heat and cook until reduced to 1/3 cup. Whisk in butter and keep warm.

Transfer salmon to a platter, or individual plates. Season to taste and pour some red wine glaze over each piece.

Spicy Shrimp in Just 2 minutes

A tasty appetizer to make the day before. Store overnight in refrigerator. The pressure cooker will infuse the shrimp with this flavorful combination of spices.

Place every ingredient in the pressure cooker and stir to mix. Lock the lid and set cooker to low, 20 kps for 2 minutes..

Quick-release to open immediately. Remove shrimp and sauce. Place in a covered dish, or Lock 'n Lock container. Chill in refrigerator for several hours.

Remove shrimp and arrange on platter. Serve with cocktail sauce for dipping.

1-1/4 cups orange juice

1-1/2 pounds large shrimp, raw, peeled, deveined, and rinsed

3-1/2 tablespoons fresh lime juice

1 teaspoon ground cumin

1 tablespoon minced garlic

1 teaspoon chili powder

Tabasco sauce to taste

1 12-ounce bottle seafood cocktail sauce

Serves 6

Halibut Steaks with Bell Peppers

This is a colorful, fresh tasting and extra moist way of preparing fish.

Set cooker to brown and add peppers, shallots and leeks. Sauté for about 5 minutes, or until vegetables start to brown. Add garlic, thyme and rosemary. Shut pressure cooker off. Place all four steaks on top of vegetables and add wine. Add salt and pepper to taste. Lock lid in place and set cooker to low, 40 kps for 4 minutes.

Quick-release pressure and test to see how well done the fish is. Halibut should flake easily. If not, let stand with lid on for a few more minutes until done. Serve the fish on top of cooked white rice with vegetables spooned on top.

Sprinkle cooking liquid on top and garnish with a fresh sprig of rosemary.

3 tablespoons vegetable oil

1 red bell pepper,
   seeded, cored and sliced
   lengthwise and cut in half

1 green bell pepper,
   seeded, cored and sliced
   lengthwise and cut in half

1 yellow bell pepper,
   seeded, cored and sliced
   lengthwise and cut in half

2 large leeks, cleaned
   and cut into 1/4 inch slices

1 clove garlic, minced

1 tablespoon fresh thyme, minced

1 tablespoon rosemary, minced

4 3/4 inch halibut steaks

1 cup dry white wine

salt and pepper to taste

4 sprigs rosemary, for garnish

Serves 4

VEGETABLE
& SIDE DISHES

Sweet-and-Sour Red Cabbage with Raspberry Jam

This recipe is on top of my list. It's an excellent side with a rich braised meat main course.

Try this easy-to-fix version, especially if you love raspberries.

Serves: 6

5 MINUTES

80 KPS **HIGH**

1 large onion, diced

1/2 pound bacon, diced

3/4 chicken broth

4 tablespoons
   raspberry vinegar,
   apple can be substituted

2 tablespoons honey

1/2 teaspoon caraway seed

1 pinch salt, just a pinch

2 pounds red cabbage,
   quartered, cored and sliced

1 6-ounce jar
   seedless raspberry jam

fresh ground
black pepper, to taste

Set the cooker to brown, add bacon and sauté until bacon has rendered it's fat and the bits have turned brown. Add the onions and sweat until translucent, about 2 minutes. Add broth and deglaze, scraping the bits from the bottom. Add vinegar, honey, caraway seeds, raspberry and salt, stir together. Add cabbage and lock lid in place. Set the cooker to high, 80 kps for 5 minutes.

Quick-release the pressure. If the cabbage is tender, let it sit in the cooker for a few minutes on warm. Add pepper to taste and serve.

Quick and Easy German Potato Salad

This is a simple way to make a delicious German potato salad at the last minute. You can use any waxy potato. My favorite is Yukon Gold.

Dress this salad with your favorite Vinaigrette dressing, homemade or store-bought.

Serves: 6

2 pounds Yukon Gold potatoes or new red or white potatoes

1 cup celery, diced

1/2 red onion, diced

2 tablespoons capers

1 cup chicken broth

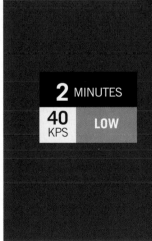

2 MINUTES

40 KPS LOW

Cut the Yukon Gold potatoes length wise and then slice into 1/4 inch slices. If using new or red potatoes, cut into four or more bite size pieces. Pour the water into the cooker. Place the potatoes in a steaming basket and place the basket in the cooker. Lock the lid in place and set the cooker to low, 40 kps for 2 minutes and let the pressure release naturally for 5 minutes and then quick-release any remaining pressure.

The potatoes should be just tender when pierced with a knife or fork. If not, leave in basket with the lid on for a couple of minutes letting the residual heat finish tenderizing the potatoes. Remove the potatoes and set aside.

Remove the cooking pot and discard the chicken stock. Return the potatoes to the cooker and add the celery, onion and capers. Add your favorite Vinaigrette and toss gently. You can keep the salad warm in the cooker until you are ready to serve.

Butternut Squash

This makes a beautiful presentation and they taste great!

Serves: 4

8 MINUTES

80 KPS **HIGH**

2 butternut squash,
   seeded and halved

1/2 cup water

4 tablespoons brown sugar

2 tablespoons butter

salt and pepper to taste

cinnamon for garnish
   and taste

Add water to cooker. Set squash on rack. Lock lid and set to high pressure, 80 kps for 8 minutes. Use natural release for 5 minutes then quick-release any remaining pressure. Remove squash. Sprinkle the brown sugar evenly into the hollow center o each squash. Add portion of butter to each center. Season to taste with salt and pepper. Sprinkle cinnamon for garnish.

Artichokes In A Hurry

Artichokes are a great appetizer. Without a pressure cooker it takes 45 minutes to steam them to tenderness. With a pressure cooker it's only 15 minutes!

Cut the stem to reveal the pale interior of each artichoke. Scrape out all the furry "choke" from the middle and snip off the thorny tops of the petals. Place artichokes in pressure cooker, wrapped in squares of heavy-duty foil on the rack. Add broth to cooker. Lock lid and set cooker to high pressure, 80 kps for 15 minutes.

Quick-release pressure. Test outer leaves for tenderness. If not tender, cook under pressure for 5 more minutes. Serve artichokes with melted butter, or a favorite dip. You can also chill artichokes and serve the next day. Check again that all the furry choke is removed from the interior of the artichoke before serving.

4 large fresh artichokes
2 cloves garlic, minced
    or 1 tbs garlic powder
olive oil
1 cup chicken broth
1 stick butter, melted

Serves 4

Garlic Potato Smash

Quick and Easy. Done in a few minutes.

In the pressure cooker combine stock, bay leaf, garlic and potatoes. Lock lid and set cooker to high, 80 kps for 6 minutes. Quick-release pressure.

Remove bay leaf. Drain off stock, reserving 1/4-cup and garlic. Add reserved liquid, milk and butter back to potatoes. Mash potatoes coarsely. Salt and pepper to taste. Serve in large bowl and garnish with parsley.

1-1/4 cups chicken broth

2 bay leaves

8 cloves garlic, sliced thin

24 new potatoes, scrubbed, cut into 1/2" chunks

1/4 cup milk

butter

salt and pepper to taste

1 tablespoon fresh parsley, minced

Serves 6

Pecan and Maple Sweet Potatoes

Maple syrup always tastes great with sweet potatoes.
The pecans add crunch and eye appeal.

Pour stock into pressure cooker and add lemon zest, brown sugar, and salt. Stir in sweet potatoes. Lock lid and set to high pressure for 5 minutes.

Quick-release pressure. Remove lid. Transfer the sweet potatoes to a serving dish with a slotted spoon.

Set cooker to brown, add butter, chopped pecans, syrup and cornstarch slurry, stirring to blend. Cook until thickened. Spoon over sweet potatoes. Garnish with whole pecans.

1 cup chicken broth

Lemon zest, from 1/2 lemon

1/2 cup brown sugar

3 medium sweet potatoes, peeled, sliced 1/2-inch thick

1/4 cup butter

1 cup pecans, coarsely chopped

1/4 cup maple syrup

1 tablespoon cornstarch mixed with 2 tbs water to form slurry

whole pecans, for garnish

Serves 6

Orange Beets

Zesty tasting easy to prepare beets.

Place cubed beets on rack in cooker. Lock lid and set cooker to high for 8 minutes. Quick-release pressure.

Remove beets and drain liquid through a colander into a bowl, reserving liquid. Set beets aside.

In cooker combine sugar and cornstarch. Set cooker to brown. Stir in orange juice and 1/4 cup reserved liquid from beets. Cook until sauce thickens and is smooth, stirring constantly. Set cooker to warm and stir in lemon juice, orange zest, and butter. Add beets and lightly toss. Hold on warm until ready to serve.

6 large beets,
   peeled and cut
   into 1/2 inch cubes

1-1/2 cups chicken broth

3 tablespoons sugar

1-1/2 tablespoons cornstarch

6 tablespoons orange juice

3 tablespoons lemon juice

orange zest from one orange

1-1/2 tablespoons butter

salt and pepper to taste

Serves 6

Broccoli with Sesame

2 MINUTES
20 KPS LOW

Great colorful and healthy side dish. If you have an electronic pressure cooker with the lowest setting of 20 kps, cook for 2 minutes. With pressure cookers with only a high and low setting, set to low and cook for 1 minute.

Pour water into cooker. Place broccoli on rack or trivet in cooker. Lock lid and set cooker to lowest possible setting, 20 kps or low. Cook at 20 kps for 2 minutes. For cookers with low setting cook for 1 minute.

Quick-release the pressure. Remove broccoli to serving dish. Sprinkle with oil, sesame seeds and salt and pepper to taste.

*To toast seeds, heat them in a non-stick skillet over medium-low heat, shaking occasionally until they're evenly golden, about 3 minutes.

1 cup water
3/4 pound broccoli spears
1/2 teaspoon sesame oil
salt and pepper to taste
1 teaspoon toasted*
   sesame seeds

Serves 4

Perfect Parsley Potatoes

Nothing could be simpler than this recipe. Done in just 6 minutes.

In a cooker combine broth and diced potatoes. Lock lid and set cooker to high, 80 kps for 6 minutes.

Quick-release pressure. Drizzle olive oil over potatoes. Toss with parsley butter and salt and pepper.

1 cup chicken broth

12 medium new red
  or white potatoes, quartered

1 teaspoon olive oil

1/4 cup fresh parsley, snipped

salt and pepper to taste

butter to taste

Serves 4

Red Potato Salad with Balsamic Dressing

Balsamic dressing is a favorite. It's perfect for these quick-cooked new potatoes.

Cut large potatoes in half and leave small ones whole. Place potatoes in steamer basket or trivet in cooker. Add 1 cup water. Lock lid and set cooker to high pressure, 80 kps for 7 minutes.

Quick-release the pressure. Drain potatoes and refresh with cold water and set aside.

For the dressing combine vinegar, mustard and Italian seasoning in a blender container or food processor. With blades spinning, slowly drizzle a thin stream of oil into the container until all the oil is emulsified and set aside. You can whisk together the same ingredients in a mixing bowl if you don't have a processor or blender. Alternatively, you can use a prepared dressing of your choice. Salt and pepper to taste.

Cut potatoes in half, place in large mixing bowl, add dressing and mix well. Gently stir in onions, dill, salt and pepper to taste. Chill until ready to serve.

3 pounds medium new
   red or white potatoes,
   washed, unpeeled
1 cup water
For Dressing:
1/4 cup red or balsamic vinegar
1 tablespoon Dijon style mustard
1/2 teaspoon Italian seasoning
1 cup extra virgin olive oil
salt and pepper to taste
2 green onions,
   sliced, whites and tops
1/4 cup chopped, fresh dill

Serves 8

Summer Ratatouille

Almost any combination of summer vegetables can be combined in a Ratatouille. This recipe has some of my favorites.

10 MINUTES

40 KPS   **LOW**

Set cooker to brown, add olive oil and heat briefly. Add eggplant and stir to coat. Add pepper, onion, zucchini, tomatoes, and garlic. Stir to mix. Add tomato paste, oregano, salt, and pepper. Stir again. Lock on lid and set to lower pressure, 40 kps for 10 minutes. Let pressure release naturally (10 minutes) to finish cooking.

Gently release any remaining pressure. Serve hot, chilled or at room temperature. Serve over hot pasta, potatoes, rice, a favorite grain or alone. Keeps in refrigerator for up to 1 week.

6 tablespoons olive oil

2 small eggplant, diced into 1/2 inch pieces

2 medium green bell peppers, seeded, cut into 1/4 inch strips

2 large onions, chunked

2 large zucchini, diced into 1/2 inch pieces

3 medium tomatoes, coarsely chopped

6 large garlic cloves, coarsely chopped

1-1/2 tablespoons tomato paste

1-1/2 teaspoons Italian spice mix

salt and pepper to taste

Serves 6

RICE & RISOTTO IN MINUTES

Risotto with Sundried Tomatoes

I love Risotto and I love the concentrated taste of Sundried Tomatoes. This combination is my favorite and in the pressure cooker total preparation and cooking time is about 10 minutes.

Serves: 6

7 MINUTES

80 KPS **HIGH**

1 tablespoon sweet butter
1 tablespoon oil from
  sundried tomatoes
2 cloves garlic, minced
1/2 cup onions, minced
1-1/2 cups Arborio rice
1 cup white wine

4 to 5 cups vegetable broth
1/2 cup sun-dried tomato, drained,
  chopped
1 cup shredded
  mozzarella cheese
salt and pepper

Set pressure cooker to brown and add butter and melt. Leaving cover off, add onions and stir until translucent but not brown, about 2 minutes. Add garlic and stir, 30 seconds. Stir in rice, coating with butter. Pour in wine and reduce for 2 minutes. Pour in 4 cups vegetable broth. Lock lid and set to high pressure, 80kps for 7 minutes.

Quick-release pressure. Remove lid and taste rice. If still not tender, add additional broth and stir. With lid removed, set the cooker to brown and stir until additional liquid is absorbed and rice is tender, 1-2 minutes. Once tender, stir in tomatoes, mozzarella, and salt and pepper to taste. Serve immediately.

Rice Pilaf
A Basic White Rice

Rice Pilaf means that the rice grains stay separate and fluffy. To achieve best results cook under pressure for 5 minutes and let rest another 5 minutes before serving. This basic white rice can be served with many of the meat recipes in this book.

Set cooker to brown and melt butter in cooker. Sauté onion until just translucent. Do not brown. Add rice and stir. Add broth and water. Lock lid and set cooker to high, 80 kps for 5 minutes. Let pressure drop naturally, about 7 minutes. Release any remaining pressure. Unlock lid. Let rice set for 5 minutes before serving.

2 tablespoons butter

1 large onion, chopped

2 cups long grain rice (not instant)

1 small can chicken broth

1-3/4 cups water

1/2 teaspoon salt

Serves 6

Risotto Primavera

Primavera means spring. Any fresh seasonal vegetable such as carrots, peas, bell peppers, broccoli and tomatoes is perfect.

Set cooker to brown, add olive oil, butter and heat. Add onions and sauté until transparent. Add garlic and rice, stirring to coat each kernel with oil. Add vegetables, wine, broth and mix well. Stir in Italian seasoning. Lock lid and set to high, 80 kps for 7 minutes.

Quick-release pressure. Remove lid and taste the rice. If not yet tender add 1/2 cup of chicken broth. Set cooker to brown and cook, stirring until broth is absorbed and rice is tender. Stir in Parmesan cheese and serve.

1 tablespoon olive oil
1 tablespoon butter
1 onion, minced
1 clove garlic, minced
1 cup short-grain rice
  (CalRose or Arborio)
1 14-1/2-ounce can vegetable
  or chicken broth
1 cup white wine
2 small carrots, chopped
1 cup broccoli flowerets
6 ounces frozen or fresh peas
1 teaspoon Italian seasoning
1/4 cup freshly grated
    Parmesan cheese

Serves 6

Shallot and Mushroom Risotto

Risotto takes on a sweeter, more subtle flavor when using shallots instead of onions.

Set cooker to brown, add olive oil and butter. Add shallots and simmer for 3 minutes, stirring often. Do not brown. Add mushrooms and rice, stirring constantly for another minute. Pour in broth and wine. Lock lid and set to high pressure, 80 kps for 7 minutes.

Quick-release pressure. Stir risotto thoroughly. Add Parmesan cheese and salt and pepper to taste.

1 tablespoon olive oil

1 tablespoon butter

2 tablespoons shallots, coarsely chopped, you can substitute onion

8 ounces fresh mushrooms, coarsely chopped

2 cups Arborio rice

4 cups vegetable broth

1 cup dry dry white wine

1/4 cup grated Parmesan cheese

salt and pepper to taste

Serves 8

Basic Wild Rice

Wild Rice is a great side dish or stuffing for many main courses. This is an easy recipe that's ready in half an hour.

Set the cooker to brown. Add butter and onions. Sauté until onions are translucent, about 3 minutes. Stir in wild rice, thoroughly coating the grains with butter. Add the remaining ingredients. Lock lid and set the cooker to high, 80 kps for 25 minutes.

Quick release the pressure. If the rice is done, each grain will be butterflied open. If most of the rice hasn't opened, lock the lid in place and cook with high pressure for an additional 5 minutes. Because wild rice varies so much it's difficult to predict exactly how long it will take to cook. Sometimes a second or third cooking is necessary.

When done, remove rice with a slotted spoon to remove excess stock and add salt and pepper to taste. Wild rice is also great as a cold side dish or served as a salad ingredient.

2 tablespoons butter
1 medium onion, chopped
1 cup wild rice
2 stalks celery
  sliced 1/8 inch thick
3 cups beef broth
1 cup mushrooms, chopped
1 bay leaf
black pepper to taste

Serves 6

Basic Brown Rice

Brown rice is perfect when you want a more earthy flavor to go along with your main course.

Set the cooker to brown and add oil. Add rice and sauté for about 2 minutes. Turn cooker off and let cool for three minutes. Meanwhile, in a separate sauce pot bring broth to a boil. Add broth to the cooker avoiding splattering if oil has not cooled properly. Lock lid and set cooker to high, 80 kps for 15 minutes. Let the pressure drop naturally, about 10 minutes.

Release any remaining pressure. Adjust moisture content if rice seems too dry. Fluff with a fork and serve right away.

1 tablespoon vegetable oil, or butter
1 cup short grained brown rice
1 can chicken or vegetable broth, boiling
1 bay leaf
1/2 teaspoon dried oregano, basil or thyme, or 1 tbs fresh
1 dash black pepper

Serves 4

BEANS
MADE EASY

How to Pressure Cook Beans

To cook dried beans in your pressure cooker you can use the pre-soak or un-soaked method. Consult the bean-cooking chart on page 102 of this book for recommended times using either method.

To pre-soak beans overnight place in a pan or bowl large enough to cover them with cold water. Pre-soaking accomplishes two things. As you see from the chart, pre-soaking cuts the cooking by several times depending upon the bean. Also, pre-soaking and discarding the soaking water reduces or eliminates the troublesome sugars that cause the flatulence associated with beans.

Some recipe writers also recommend a quick-soak method of cooking beans for a few minutes under pressure and then quick releasing the pressure. I never recommend this method because quick releasing causes the skins of the beans to wrinkle and sometimes separate from the beans. I don't like this look and I don't like the possibility of the skins blocking one or more of the safety valves of your cooker.

When following the times recommended on the bean chart remember that all beans are different because of age, dryness and hardness. It may be necessary to cook beans a few minutes longer to achieve the desired tenderness. Because you will be using the natural release method if you add additional time, usually only 3 to 5 minutes additional time is necessary to soften even the toughest old bean.

New Orleans Red Beans and Rice

An everyday meal in a lot of cultures because it's simple, delicious and inexpensive.

Serves: 8

15 MINUTES

80 KPS **HIGH**

2 cups dried red kidney beans

2 teaspoons olive oil

1 large onion, chopped

2 large carrots, peeled and diced

5 cloves garlic, minced

1 stalk celery, diced

1 14-ounce can diced tomatoes

1 teaspoon Tabasco sauce

1 dried bay leaf

1 smoked ham hock

2 cups water

2 cups chicken broth

1/2 pound smoked sausages,
    Andouile if you like a little bite

3 cups cooked white rice
    follow recipe for basic white rice

salt and pepper to taste

Rinse the beans in a colander under cold water, check to make sure no stones or gravel remain and throw away any darkened or shriveled beans. Soak them using either the overnight or quick-soak method discussed at the beginning of this chapter.

Set the cooker to brown and add the olive oil, onion and garlic. Cook briefly about 2 minutes stirring constantly, you do not want to brown the onions or the garlic, only soften until they turn translucent. Add the carrots, celery, tomatoes, Tabasco Sauce and bay leaf. Cook for another two minutes stirring. Add the beans, ham hock, water and stock. Lock the lid in place, set the cooker to high, 80 kps and cook for 15 minutes. Release the pressure naturally.

Unlock and remove the lid. Add the sausage, set the cooker to brown and cook with the lid off for two minutes. Remove the ham hock and discard the bone and skin. Cut the meat into bite size bits and add back to the beans. Crush a spoonful of beans against the side of the cooker and stir. This will release enough starch to thicken the bean mixture just a bit. Season to taste and serve with the white rice.

Bean-n-Sausage Dinner

Navy beans are good by themselves but the addition of sausage completes a meal served with a nice green salad.

Rinse beans in a colander and remove stones and discolored beans. Soak overnight, or use quick-pressure soak method described at beginning of this chapter.

Set cooker to brown, add oil and sauté onion and garlic, 2 to 3 minutes or until onion is translucent. Stir frequently to prevent onion from browning. Add carrot, celery, sage, sausage, beans, stock, and water. Stir well. Add enough water so it's at least 2 inches above beans. Lock lid and set to high, 80 kps for 15 minutes.

Be sure and release pressure naturally, about 10 minutes.

2 cups dry navy beans
1 teaspoon olive oil
1 small onion, finely chopped
1 clove garlic, minced
1 pound Italian sausage
   cut into bite size pieces
1 small carrot, peeled, diced
1 stalk celery, diced
1/4 teaspoon dried sage
3 cups beef broth
2 cups water
salt and pepper to taste

Serves 6

Orange Baked Blackeyed Peas

This dish has great flavor. Beans absorb varying amounts of water and thicken upon standing, so you may need to adjust by adding or draining off excess liquid to achieve desired texture.

Set cooker to brown, add bacon and sauté until browned. Drain off fat. Add beans and remaining ingredients. Add water to cover beans, making sure cooker is no more than 1/2 full. Lock lid and set cooker to high, 80 kps for 30 minutes.

Naturally release pressure. Let stand for a few minutes. Adjust moisture with water or orange juice to achieve desired texture.

2 cups blackeyed peas
1/4 pound bacon, diced
1 cup orange juice
1/2 cup ketchup
2 tablespoons molasses
2 tablespoons sherry or vinegar
2 teaspoons salt
1/2 teaspoon dry mustard
1/4 teaspoon ginger

Serves 6

Basic Beans in Broth

Cooking beans from scratch is quick and easy in a pressure cooker. This is a basic recipe without having to soak the beans overnight. Consult the bean cooking chart for individual bean cooking times.

Combine every ingredient in the cooker, including salt to hold the skin intact during cooking. Set the cooker to high, 80 kps for the indicated time on the bean cooking chart. Always allow the pressure to come down naturally. Never quick-release beans because it causes the skin to loosen.

Test the beans for tenderness. They should have a creamy texture and mash easily. If not done, simmer on brown with the lid off for a few more minutes. Allow beans to cool in the cooker so they'll remain firm and not break apart when drained.

Drain in batches and be careful not to pile up so the beans will remain intact. You may refrigerate the beans for up to five days before serving.

Remember to keep and refrigerate the bean cooking liquid as a flavorful cooking stock to be used within the next few days.

2-1/2 cups dried beans
10 cups water
3/4 teaspoon salt
1 tablespoon vegetable oil
4 cloves garlic, peeled
2 bay leaves
1 large carrot,
   cut into 3 or 4 pieces
1 stalk celery,
   cut into 3 or 4 pieces

Serves 8

Lentils
Basic Recipe

Lentils make a great side dish or base for serving a variety of main courses. I love the steamed salmon with raspberry glaze served on top of lentils.

Add the lentils, bay leaf, garlic, onion, oil, wine and water to the cooker. Lock lid in place and set pressure to high, 80 kps for 7 minutes. Quick-release pressure.

Check to make sure lentils are done. If not, re-lock lid and return to full pressure, cooking for 1 to 2 minutes. Remove bay leaf. Drain off most of the liquid. Stir in mustard, parsley and season to taste.

2 cups dried lentils,
  picked over, rinsed

1 bay leaf

2 cloves garlic, minced

1 large onion, coarsely chopped

1 tablespoon vegetable oil

1/2 cup white wine

5 cups water

3 tablespoons Dijon style
  mustard, or prepared mustard

1/3 cup fresh parsley, minced

salt and pepper to taste

Serves 6

Refried Beans

This is a zesty version including browned onions, lime juice and zest.

Set the cooker to brown. Add oil, onions, and cumin. Sauté until onions are slightly browned. Add garlic and oregano and sauté for one more minute, stirring constantly. Stir in one cup of bean cooking liquid or chicken stock and half of the cooked beans.

Use a potato masher and mash to desired consistency, mashed smooth or with broken pieces. When the cooking liquid is absorbed turn off the cooker. Stir in cheese and add lime juice, zest and salt and pepper to taste.

3-1/2 cups cooked red, black
    or white kidney beans,
    or pinto beans.
Follow directions for basic beans,
you will need about 1/2 cups
dried beans

1 tablespoon vegetable oil

1 large onion, chopped

1 teaspoon whole cumin seeds,
    or 1/2 tsp dried ground cumin

1 clove garlic, minced

1/2 teaspoon dried oregano

1 cup bean cooking liquid, or
    chicken or vegetable stock

1/2 cup jalapeno jack cheese
    grated, plus more for garnish

3 tablespoons lime juice,
    added to taste

1/2 teaspoon lemon zest

salt and pepper to taste

Serves 6

Quick & Easy Desserts

Decadent Chocolate Cheesecake

Who doesn't like chocolate? It's especially wonderful in this creamy chocolate cheesecake. Plan to make this dessert a day ahead and refrigerate to firm before serving.

Serves: 6

1 cup chocolate wafer
   cookie crumbs

2 tablespoons butter, melted

2 8-ounce packages
   cream cheese, softened

1/2 cup sweetened condensed milk

3 eggs

1-1/2 cups semisweet
   chocolate chips, melted

1 teaspoon vanilla extract

2-1/2 cups water

1 Heath bar, crumbled

20 MINUTES

80 KPS HIGH

...ghtly butter a 7-inch springform pan. Cover the outside of the pan with ...heet of aluminum foil. Combine cookie crumbs and melted butter, stir together ...en press the mixture into the bottom of pan, about 1 inch high.

...a large mixing bowl, use an electric mixer on medium speed and blend until the mixture is fluffy. Add ...nilla extract to the melted chocolate and mix until well blended. Pour the mixture over the crust in the ...n. Cover the springform pan with it's cover or aluminum foil. Pour water into the cooker and place a ...etal trivet or steamer rack on the bottom. Place the springform pan on the trivet.

...ck lid in place, set the cooker to high, 80 kps for 20 minutes. Allow pressure to release naturally, about ...minutes. Release any remaining pressure with the quick-release. Unlock and remove cover.

...move cheesecake from pressure cooker, set aside on a rack, let cool to room temperature and refrigerate ...ernight. Crumble the Heath bar by smashing it against the counter top while it's still in the wrapper. ...move the sides of the spring form pan, sprinkle the top with the crumbled Heath bar and serve.

Bread Pudding with Brown Sugar

If you have regular, old white bread that's past it's prime, this is a great way to use it.

Butter bread with 2 tablespoons butter. Cut into 1-1/2 inch cubes. Sprinkle brown sugar evenly in bottom of a 7-inch bundt pan, or other heat-proof dish that'll fit easily into the cooker. Cut remaining 2 tablespoons butter into small pieces and dot over sugar. Sprinkle with brandy. Add cubed bread, but don't stir. In a mixing bowl, whisk half and half with eggs, egg yolks, vanilla and pinch of salt. Pour over bread but don't stir. Cover dish with lid or aluminum foil, tightly to keep dry.

Pour two cups water into pressure cooker. Set rack in cooker. Place bundt pan or baking dish in steamer basket (or foil sling) and lower into cooker. The water should cover the lower third of the pan or dish. Lock lid and set cooker to high, 80 kps for 20 minutes.

Release pressure naturally. Let rest for 5 minutes then remove baking dish. Pour off any accumulated water from the lid top before removing. Serve immediately.

4 slices day old white bread, make sure it is dry

4 tablespoons sweet cream butter, divided

1 cup brown sugar, packed

1 tablespoon brandy or 1 teaspoon brandy extract

1-1/2 cups half and half

2 large eggs

2 large egg yolks

1 teaspoon vanilla extract

pinch salt

2 cups water

Serves 6

Rice Pudding with Honey and Raisins

Rice Pudding was never easier.

Combine rice, olive oil, and water in cooker. Lock lid and set cooker to high, 80 kps for 10 minutes.

Quick-release pressure. Stir in honey and sugar. Add evaporated milk, milk and egg yolks. Set cooker to brown and cook for 3 minutes or until mixture thickens, stirring constantly. Add raisins and vanilla extract.

Spoon into dishes and sprinkle with cinnamon. Serve hot or cold.

1-1/2 cups long grain rice
3/4 teaspoon olive oil
3 cups water
1/2 cup honey
3/4 cup sugar
1 cup evaporated milk
6 tablespoons milk
4 1/2 egg yolks
1/2 cup raisins
1-1/2 teaspoons vanilla extract
cinnamon, to taste

Serves 6

Grand Marnier Bread Pudding with Trail Mix

This recipe is a variation from my friend, Lorna Sass with the exception of trail mix substituted for dried fruit. When I couldn't find a package of mixed dried fruit, I used what I had and liked the additional crunch of the mixed nuts and seeds.

Coat the inside of a 7 inch bundt pan with butter. Butter the dried bread slices. Cut each slice into 4 pieces. Arrange 1/3 of the slices as a bottom layer in the pan.

In a mixing bowl, use a whisk to combine the milk, Grand Marnier, eggs, honey, orange zest and nutmeg. Pour 1/3 of the mixture over the first layer of bread. Turn the bread pieces over to thoroughly absorb the mixture. Distribute 1/3 of the trail mix on top of the first layer of bread. Repeat this procedure with the bread, liquified mixture and trail mix twice more.

Place cover, or foil on top of bundt pan. Place a trivet in the bottom of the cooker. Set the bundt pan on top of the rack. Carefully add enough water to 1/3 height of the pan. Lock lid and set the cooker to high, 80 kps for 15 minutes.

Let the pressure drop naturally, about 10 minutes. Remove lid and let the pudding cool for 5 minutes before removing from the cooker. If you're not serving immediately, set the cooker to warm and set lid ajar, or cut holes in the foil until you're ready to serve. Garnish with cinnamon.

15 MINUTES
80 KPS HIGH

3 tablespoons butter

8 thick slices white Italian or French bread left out 24 hours to dry

1-2/3 cups milk

1/3 cup Grand Marnier

4 large eggs, beaten

1/4 cup honey

2 tablespoons orange zest

1/8 teaspoon nutmeg freshly grated

1-1/2 cups trail mix or dried fruits and nuts

cinnamon for garnish

Serves 6

Applesauce Made Easy

Once you've made homemade applesauce you'll never want to go back to canned or bottled. When I use red apples I prefer them un-peeled for the rosy color and delicious flavor. Add sweetener after cooking and make it as sweet as you like.

Add water, apples and lemon juice to the cooker. Lock the lid and set the cooker to high, 80 kps for 10 minutes. Let the pressure release naturally, about 10 minutes.

Remove lid and let the cooked apples cool slightly. Pass apples through a food mill. Adjust the flavor by sweetening to your liking. You can refrigerate up to two weeks. This applesauce is great with roast pork.

1 cup water
3 pounds apples
1 tablespoon lemon juice
sugar, honey or
artificial sweetener

Serves 6

Cranapple Sauce

Perfect with roast turkey. You can't buy this sauce in the store.

Add water, cranberries, apples and lemon juice to the cooker. Lock the lid and set the cooker to high, 80 kps for 10 minutes. Let the pressure release naturally, about 10 minutes.

Remove lid and let cooked apples cool slightly. Pass apples through a food mill. Adjust flavor by sweetening to your preference. You can refrigerate up to two weeks. I love this sauce with roast turkey.

1 cup water
2-1/2 pounds apples
2 cups fresh cranberries
1 tablespoon lemon juice
sugar, honey or
artificial sweetener

Serves 6

Vegetable Cooking Chart

Vegetable	Approximate Cooking time in Minutes	Standard Pressure Cooker, High or Low Quick-Release	Approximate Cooking time in Minutes	Adjustable Electronic Pressure Cooker KPS Quick-Release
Artichoke, large whole, without leaves	10	High	10	80
Artichoke, medium whole, without leaves	7	High	7	80
Artichoke, small whole, without leaves	5	High	5	80
Artichoke, hearts	3	Low	6	40
Asparagus, fine, whole	1	Low	2	20
Asparagus, thick, whole	2	Low	3	20
Beans, green, whole (fresh or frozen)	2	Low	4	40
Beets, 1/4" (5 mm) slices	5	High	5	80
Beet greens	1	Low	2	40
Beans, yellow, whole (fresh or frozen)	2	Low	4	40
Broccoli, flowerets	2	Low	3	20
Broccoli, stalks	5	High	5	80
Broccoli, stalks, 1/4" (5 mm) slices	3	Low	4	40
Brussel sprouts, whole	4	Low	5	40
Cabbage, red or green, in quarters	3	Low	4	40
Cabbage, red or green, 1/4" (5 mm) slices	1	Low	1	40
Carrots, 1/4" (5 mm) slices	1	Low	2	40
Carrots, 1" (25 mm) chunks	4	Low	5	40
Cauliflower flowerets	2	Low	3	40
Celery, 1" (25 mm) chunks	3	Low	4	40
Collard	5	High	5	80
Corn, kernels	1	Low	1	40
Corn on the cob	2	Low	3	40
Eggplant, 1/4" (5 mm) slices	3	Low	4	40
Eggplant, 1/2" (10 mm) chunks	3	Low	4	40
Endive, thickly cut	1	Low	2	20
Escarole, coarsely chopped	1	Low	2	20
Green beans, whole (fresh or frozen)	2	Low	3	40
Kale, coarsely chopped	2	Low	3	20

Vegetable Cooking Chart

Vegetable	Approximate Cooking time in Minutes	Standard Pressure Cooker, High or Low Quick-Release	Approximate Cooking time in Minutes	Adjustable Electronic Pressure Cooker KPS Quick-Release
Leeks (white part)	3	Low	4	40
Mixed vegetables, frozen	2	Low	3	40
Okra, small pods	2	Low	3	40
Onions, medium whole	2	Low	3	40
Parsnips, 1/4" (5 mm) slices	1	Low	1	20
Parsnips, 1" (25 mm) slices	3	Low	4	40
Peas, in the pod	1	Low	2	20
Peas, green	1	Low	2	20
Potatoes, cut into 1" (25 mm) cubes	5	High	5	80
Potatoes, new, whole small	5	High	5	80
Potatoes, whole large	10	High	10	80
Pumpkin, 2" (50 mm) slices	4	High	4	80
Red beet, in 1/4" (5 mm) slices	4	High	4	80
Red beet, large, whole	20	High	20	80
Red beet, small, whole	12	High	12	80
Rutabaga, 1/2" (10 mm) slices	4	High	4	80
Rutabaga, 1" (25 mm) chunks	5	High	5	80
Spinach, fresh	1	Low	1	20
Spinach, frozen	4	Low	5	40
Squash, acorn, halved	7	Low	8	40
Squash, butternut, 1" (25 mm) slices	4	Low	5	40
Sweet potato, 1 1/2" (40 mm) slices	5	Low	6	40
Swiss chard	2	Low	3	40
Tomatoes, in quarters	2	Low	3	40
Tomatoes, whole	3	High	3	80
Turnip, small, in quarters	3	Low	4	40
Turnip, in 1 1/2" (40 mm) slices	3	Low	4	40
Yellow beans, whole (fresh or frozen)	2	Low	3	40
Zucchini, 1/4" (5 mm) slices	1	Low	1	20

Meat and Poultry Cooking Chart

Meat/Poultry	Brown	Weight Pounds	Liquid Minimum	Cooking Time	High = 80 kps Natural Release
Beef, brisket, fresh or corned		2 to 3	cover	45	High
Beef, brisket, fresh or corned		4 to 5	cover	70	High
Beef, flank steak	Yes	2 to 3	1 cup	35	High
Beef, ground	Yes	1 to 2	2-Jan	6	High
Beef. heart		3 to 4	cover	75	High
Beef, kidney			cover	10	High
Beef, liver, sliced			2 cups	5	High
Beef Oxtails	Yes		cover	45	High
Beef, pot roast	Yes	3 to 4	2 cups	60	High
Beef, rib roast	Yes	3 to 4	2 cups	60	High
Beef or Veal Shanks	Yes		1 1/2 cups	45	High
Beef, Short Ribs	Yes		1 1/2 cups	100	High
Beef Stew meat	Yes	1 1/2" cubes	1 cup	30	High
Chicken, breasts with bone	Yes		1/2 cup	10	High
Chicken, breasts boneless	Yes		1/2 cup	5	High
Chicken, legs or thighs	Yes		1/2 cup	5 to 7	High
Chicken, stewing		4 to 6	cover	40	High
Chicken, wings			1/2 cup	6	High
Chicken, whole	Yes	3 to 4	2 cups	30	High
Ham Hocks			Cover	60	High
Ham, fully cooked		4 to 6	3 cups	40	High
Lamb, breast	Yes	2 to 3	2 cups	40	High
Lamb, chops 1/2 inch thick	Yes		1/2 cup	5	High
Lamb, chops 1 inch thick	Yes		1/2 cup	12	High
Lamb, leg	Yes	3 to 5	2 cups	30 to 45	High
Lamb, shanks	Yes		1 1/2 cups	45	High
Pork, chops 1/2 inch thick	Yes		1/2 cup	7	High
Pork, chops 1 inch thick	Yes		1/2 cup	15	High
Pork, loin	Yes	3 to 5	2 cups	50	High
Pork, spareribs, baby back			1 cup	15	High
Pork, roasts, any cut	Yes	3 to 5	2 cups	30 to 45	High
Turkey, breast boneless	Yes	3 to 5	2 cups	25	High
Turkey, breast bone in	Yes	4 to 6	2 cups	30	High
Veal Shanks	Yes		1 1/2 cups	45	High
Venison, roast any cut	Yes	4 to 6	2 cups	40	High

Bean Cooking Chart

Bean	Soaked Natural Release Cooking Time in Minutes	Unsoaked Natural Release Cooking Time in Minutes	Recommended Pressure High = 80 kps
Adzuki	2	16	High
Anasazi	2	18	High
Beans, black	4	20	High
Beans, garbanzo (chickpeas)	10	35	High
Beans, great northern	8	25	High
Beans, lima, baby	3	12	High
Beans, lima, large	3	12	High
Beans, navy or pea or white (haricot)	4	20	High
Beans, pinto	3	22	High
Beans, red kidney	8	22	High
Beans, soy (beige)	8	28	High
Beans, soy (black)	16	35	High
Beans, white kidney (cannellini)	8	35	High
Chickpeas (chick peas, garbanzo bean or kabuli)	14	35	High
Cranberry (romano or borlotti)	8	30	High
Gandules (pigeon peas)	5	20	High
Lentils, French green	na	8	High
Lentils, green, mini (brown)	na	6	High
Lentils, red, split	na	4	High
Lentils, yellow, split (moong dal)	na	4	High
Peas, split, green or yellow	na	6	High
Peas, dried, whole	6	12	High
Peas, black eyed	na	8	High
Scarlet runner	10	16	High

Rice Cooking Chart

Rice	Grain : Water Ratio Cups	Yield in Cups	Cooking time in Minutes	Pressure High = 80 kps Natural Release
White Rice, Long Grain: Basmati, Jasmine, Texmat	1 cup rice to 1 1/2 cups water	2 1/2 cups	4	High
Risotto White Rice, Arborio, Carnaroli, Maratelli	1 cup rice to 4 to 5 cups stock	7 to 8 cups	4	High
Brown Rice	1 cup rice to 1 3/4 cups water	2 1/2 cups	15	High
Wild Rice (Indian Water Grass)	1 cup rice to 3 cups broth	4 cups	22	High